M 12/06

TUDORS, STUARTS & CIVIL WAR

TUDORS, STUARTS & CIVIL WAR

Philip Steele

Miles Kelly

PUBLISHING

First published in 2002 by Miles Kelly Publishing Ltd,
Bardfield Centre, Great Bardfield, Essex, CM7 4SL

ISBN 1-84236-143-0

2 4 6 8 10 9 7 5 3 1

Some material in this book can also be found
in the *Encyclopedia of British History*
Project Manager: Kate Miles
Art Director: Clare Sleven
Artwork Commissioning: Janice Bracken & Lesley Cartlidge
Picture Research: Ruth Boardman
Referencing: Liberty Newton
Assistant: Lisa Clayden
Repro: DPI

Contact us by email: info@mileskelly.net
Website: www.mileskelly.net

Printed in Hong Kong

CONTENTS

İNTRODUCTİON

Five hundred years ago the people of the British Isles, like others in western Europe, began to venture overseas. Ships were now sailing for the New World of the Americas, for Africa and Asia. Adventurers were seizing new lands and trading in furs, timber, gold and soon also in a shameful human cargo – slaves. Merchants and bankers became richer and the middle classes became more powerful.

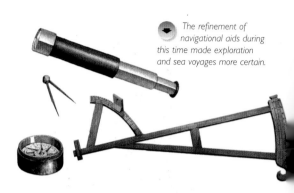

The refinement of navigational aids during this time made exploration and sea voyages more certain.

In Europe there was a revival of learning and the arts, which became known as the Renaissance or 'rebirth'. Scientific research was beginning to change the way in which people saw the world and the universe. In Britain, the 1500s and 1600s saw the plays of William Shakespeare, the poetry of John Milton, and the scientific work of Isaac Newton.

In northern Europe people called Protestants rebelled against the Catholic Church, resulting in changes in the way people worshipped (the Reformation) and in fierce religious wars. Religious conflict spread through the British Isles, too.

By 1542 England was united with Wales. Both were ruled by the Tudor royal family. Scotland was ruled by the Stuarts, and in 1603 King James VI of Scotland bcame James I of England. The two thrones were united, although the two parliaments were not joined until in 1707. In Ireland, British monarchs tried to extend their rule beyond the Dublin area, by settlement and invasion.

The 1600s saw the rulers of Britain become increasingly out of touch with their subjects. The Stuart kings often treasted Parliament with

The reign of Elizabeth I (1558-1603) saw the flourishing of commerce, exploration, science and the arts.

Isaac Newton (1642-1727) was a remarkable physicist and mathematician. Two of his great discoveries were the law of gravity and the creation of calculus.

was becoming ever weaker, while the rule of law and parliament was becoming ever stronger.

What do these great events mean to us today? The 1500s marked the end of the Middle Ages in the British Isles. In the 200 years that followed we see the development of Parliament, the union of nations, the seeds of trouble in Ireland and the start of Britain's involvement in Africa, Asia and the Americas. We see the foundations of modern Britain and Ireland being laid.

contempt and in 1642 triggered off a civil war. In 1649 King Charles I was executed and Parliament ruled, later handing over power to one man, Oliver Cromwell.

By 1660 the Stuart kings were back in power, but with their powers now limited by law. Religious strife led to Catholic James II fleeing the land and the throne being offered jointly to his Protestant daughter Mary and the Dutch ruler William of Orange. The power of kings

Leisure time may well have been spent at open air fairs. Here crowds gather by the river to enjoy dancing, sports, entertainments and food.

The English Civil War took place in the middle of the 17th century between the king and the Royalists (Cavaliers) on one side and the Parliamentarians (Roundheads) on the other.

PALACES AND PLAYERS

1509–1714

THE WORLD AT A GLANCE

ELSEWHERE IN EUROPE

1512
Michelangelo completes painting of the Sistine Chapel, in Rome

1517
German monk Martin Luther starts the Protestant Reformation

1571
Naval Battle of Lepanto, Christian fleet led by Venice defeats the Turks

1618
Religious strife in the Holy Roman Empire leads to the Thirty Years War

1643
Louis XIV the 'Sun King' becomes ruler of France

1648
Spain recognizes independence of the Netherlands, art and trade flourish

1701
Frederick I becomes first King of Prussia, in east Germany

1703
Peter the Great, Tsar of Russia, builds new capital at St Petersburg

ASIA

1526
Babar defeats Delhi and founds the Moghul empire in northern India

1566
The Ottoman (Turkish) empire is at its greatest extent

1581
The Russians begin their conquest of Siberia (northeast Asia)

1587
Abbas I 'the Great' rules Persia, a golden age of arts and crafts

1603
Tokugawa Ieyasu becomes Shogun, brings all Japan under his rule

1619
The Dutch found colonial empire in the East Indies, based at Djakarta

1644
Manchurian emperors now rule China: the Qing dynasty

1707
The death of Emperor Aurangzeb, decline of Moghusl power in India

AFRICA

1546
Songhai destroys the empire of Mali in West Africa

1517
Egypt is conquered by the Turks and becomes part of the Ottoman empire

1575
Portuguese found Luanda and settle the coast of Angola

1578
Moroccans defeat Portuguese in North Africa

1600
The Oyo state is at the height of its power in Nigeria

1632
Emperor Fasilidas closes Ethiopia to foreigners

1662
Portuguese defeat the kingdom of Kongo, southern Central Africa

1700
Rise of Ashanti power in Ghana, West Africa

"New faiths, new nations and faraway lands..."

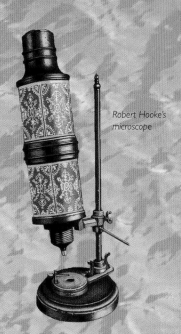

Robert Hooke's microscope

NORTH AMERICA

1510
First African slaves begin to arrive in North America

1519
Spanish begin conquest of Aztec empire in Mexico

1570
Northeast Native Americans form an alliance, the Iroquois Confederacy

1607
English found a permanent settlement at Jamestown, Virginia

1608
French colonists found a settlement at Québec, in Canada

1625
Dutch settle New Amsterdam (later New York City)

1684
French explore the Mississippi region and claim Louisiana

1692
Port Royal, Jamaica, a notorious pirate haven, is destroyed by earthquake

SOUTH AMERICA

1519
Portuguese Ferdinand Magellan explores the Strait named after him

1532
The Spanish invade and defeat the Inca empire of Peru

1536
The first Spanish settlement at Buenos Aires, Argentina

1541
The Spanish found a settlement at Santiago, in Chile

1545
Spanish develop silver mining in the Andes mountains

1560
The Portuguese lay out sugarcane plantations in Brazil

1620
Dutch West India Company settles Guyana, northern South America

1667
Dutch colonists take Suriname, in northern South America

OCEANIA

1519
Portuguese explorer Ferdinand Magellan enters the Pacific Ocean

1526
Portuguese explorer Jorge de Menezes visits New Guinea

1600
Decline of Easter Island culture due to over-population and warfare

1600
Tu'i Kanokupolu dynasty comes to power in Hawaiian islands

1606
Dutch explorer Willem Jansz sights Cape York Peninsula, Australia

1616
Dutch crew under Dirck Hartog lands in Western Australia

1642
Dutch explorer Abel Tasman reaches Tasmania and New Zealand

1643
Tasman sails to the Pacific islands of Tonga and Fiji

10

1509
Henry VIII marries Catherine of Aragon (Spain).

1512
Henry VIII claims French throne. War with France.

1520
English-French meeting at Field of the Cloth of Gold

1530
Wolsey falls from power over divorce crisis

1533
Henry VIII marries Anne Boleyn

KING HARRY'S DAYS

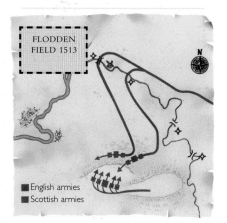

FLODDEN FIELD 1513

N

■ English armies
■ Scottish armies

YOUNG Henry VIII, crowned King of England in 1509, loved to fight tournaments in gleaming armour. In 1520 he met François I of France at the Field of the Cloth of Gold, near Calais. Both sides wore the most splendid clothes imaginable. Standards fluttered in front of luxurious tents. However although royal courts still dreamed of chivalry, the period we call the Middle Ages had already slipped away.

In 1513, while Henry VIII was away fighting in France, the Scots invaded England. They were defeated at Flodden. Ten thousand were killed, including James IV, who was married to Henry's sister Margaret.

Henry VIII's personal life led to an historic break with the Church of Rome.

THE EARLY TUDORS

Henry VII had been a skillful ruler, who survived false claims to the throne and rebellions over his harsh taxation. His sickly eldest son, Arthur, died young. However his second son, who became Henry VIII, was strong and energetic. In the new Europe, nations were competing for power and trade. Henry was a cunning statesman, as was his Lord Chancellor, a bullying, arrogant churchman called Thomas Wolsey.

THE KING WITH SIX WIVES

The young Henry VIII cut a fine figure, but by the time of his death in 1547 he had become bloated, overweight and diseased. He married no fewer than six times. His marriages were marked by passion, political intrigue, jealousy, rage and selfishness. Henry's love for a beautiful courtier called Anne Boleyn led him to demand a divorce from Catherine of Aragon. The Pope refused and this led to a crisis which changed the direction of English history.

MONEY, LAND AND SHEEP

While Henry VIII spent lavishly on court life and on wars, ordinary people suffered extreme hardship. The Spanish were now mining gold and silver in the Americas, and this upset the economy of other European countries.

Prices began to rise and rents with them. For many years common land, that had always been used by the public for farming and grazing, was seized by greedy landlords. Many poor people were forced off the land, to become beggars and outlaws.

In July 1549 Robert Kett, from Wymondham in Norfolk, led a rebellion against the enclosure of common land for sheep pasture. Kett attracted 16,000 supporters to his cause and they killed 20,000 sheep as a protest. They occupied the city of Norwich, but Kett was captured and hanged.

The Guildhall at Lavenham in Norfolk, East Anglia, was built in 1529. Lavenham was a centre of the wool trade and wool was the mainstay of the English economy.

DIVORCE AND REBELLION

When Henry VIII demanded something, he usually got it. Thomas Wolsey was unable to persuade Pope Clement VII to agree to Henry's divorce with Catherine of Aragon, so he was thrown out of office. In 1534 a law was passed making Henry VIII head of the Church in England, so that he could decide his own fate. The arrogance of the king and his officials led to many uprisings. In 1536-37 there was a major rebellion in Yorkshire and Lincolnshire, called the Pilgrimage of Grace.

RULERS OF ENGLAND

House of Tudor (continued)
✦ Henry VIII   1509-1547
✦ Edward VI   1547-1553
✦ Mary I   1553-1558
✦ Elizabeth I   1558-1603

Catherine of Aragon was the widow of Prince Arthur. Henry demanded a divorce.

Henry married Anne Boleyn in 1533, but they quarrelled and she was executed in 1536.

Henry married Jane Seymour the day after Anne was executed. She died in childbirth.

The fourth marriage was for political reasons and Henry found Anne of Cleves too unattractive.

After another divorce, Henry married Catherine Howard, but executed her too, for being unfaithful.

Henry's sixth wife, Catherine Parr, was a wise queen, who survived Henry's death.

● 1517
Martin Luther starts
Protestant movement in
Germany

● 1521
Henry VIII is made Defender
of the Faith by the Pope

● 1531
English priests recognise
Henry VIII as head of the
Church in England

● 1534
Henry VIII breaks ties with
the Church of Rome

● 1535
Thomas Cromwell starts
to seize Church wealth for
the state

CLASHES ⊙ OF FAITH

I N 1521, Pope Leo X had honoured Henry VIII of England with the title 'Defender of the Faith', because of his support for the Roman Church. Within 13 years, however, Henry had broken with Rome and made himself head of the Church in England – all because of his divorce with Catherine of Aragon. This marked the start of centuries of religious conflict in the British Isles.

The English nursery rhyme 'Little Jack Horner' has its origins in history. Horner was steward to the Abbot of Glastonbury. When Henry VIII was busy seizing the wealth of the monasteries, Horner stole the deeds (ownership papers) to a manor house called Mells, in Somerset, and gave them to Henry VIII. The 'good boy' was rewarded with the land – a real 'plum'. The last abbot of Glastonbury, Robert Whiting, was executed in 1539.

THOMAS MORE'S *UTOPIA*

Thomas More's perfect land of Utopia was far removed from the realities of Henry VIII's England

Sir Thomas More was appointed Lord Chancellor of England in 1529. He did not want the job, but he carried it out dutifully. Although More wished to see many changes in the Roman Church, he refused to accept Henry VIII as head of the English Church. More was beheaded for treason in 1535. In 1516 More wrote a book in Latin, which compared the social problems of his day with an imagined island where there was an ideal society. The name of the book was *Utopia* – from the Greek words for 'nowhere'.

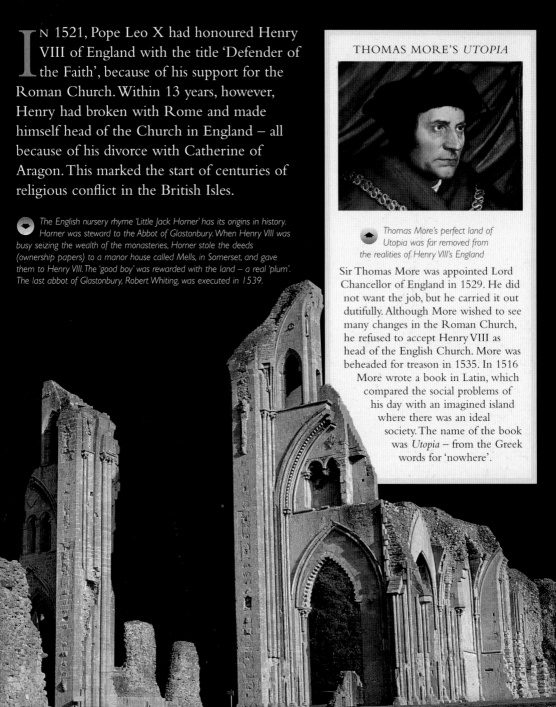

⚙ **1535**
Thomas More is executed on
Tower Hill, London

⚙ **1535**
First complete Bible in English

⚙ **1539**
The Dissolution of the
Monasteries approved by
parliament

⚙ **1540**
Lutherans persecuted in
England

⚙ **1547**
John Knox starts the
Reformation in Scotland

13

THE PROTESTANTS

New ideas were entering the British Isles from mainland
Europe during the reign of Henry VIII. They came from
people who were known as Protestants, because they
were protesting against the Roman 'Catholic' (meaning
'universal') Church, its teachings and its customs. Leading
Protestant campaigners included a German called Martin
Luther and a Frenchman called John Calvin. Their
demands for reform led to this period of European
history being called the Reformation.

*The year 1539 saw the 'dissolution' (closing down) of
Roman Catholic monasteries in England and Wales.
The property was mostly sold off to nobles, raising huge
amounts of money for Henry VIII. The operation was
organized by Thomas Cromwell, another powerful politican
who ended up having his head chopped off.*

*The early Tudor period produced some beautiful
church architecture. The roof of King's College
Chapel, Cambridge, fans out into a delicate tracery of
stone. It was completed in 1515.*

AN ENGLISH CHURCH

Henry VIII broke with Rome for political
reasons, rather than because of his religious
beliefs. He had little sympathy for the
English supporters of Martin Luther and
intended the English Church to follow basic
Catholic teachings. During the reign of
Henry's successor, Edward VI, the Church in
England did adopt Protestant policies.

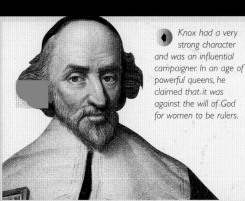

*Knox had a very
strong character
and was an influential
campaigner. In an age of
powerful queens, he
claimed that it was
against the will of God
for women to be rulers.*

THE SCOTTISH REFORMER

John Knox was born at
Haddington, Lothian, in
about 1513. He became
a Catholic priest in 1540,
but soon fell under the
influence of the Lutheran
George Wishart. Wishart
was burnt for his beliefs
in 1547, and Knox
became a Protestant
minister. He spent some

time in England in the
service of Edward VI and
then went to Switzerland,
where he studied the
teachings of John Calvin.
Knox returned to
Scotland in 1559. Despite
the efforts of the Scottish
Catholics, a Protestant
Church of Scotland was
recognized in 1560.

14

⚙ 1498
Henry VII rebuilds palace at
Richmond, Surrey

⚙ 1515
Thomas Wolsey builds
Hampton Court palace

⚙ 1526
German artist Hans Holbein
makes portraits of the
Tudor court

⚙ 1533
Anne Boleyn gives birth to
Elizabeth at Greenwich palace

⚙ 1536
St James's Palace is built in
London

A TUDOR PALACE

I N Tudor times, the River Thames was the lifeline of the growing city of London. Rowing boats called wherries carried passengers across to the south bank and sometimes a splendid royal barge could be seen, its oars dipping in the water. It would leave the royal landing stage by Whitehall Palace and beat upstream to the royal palaces at Richmond or Hampton Court, or downstream to the grand palace of Greenwich.

The court of Henry VIII followed French fashions, with rich velvets, satins and brocades for both men and women.

LIVING IN LUXURY

Nobles no longer lived in draughty castles. They built fine country houses, often of brick, surrounded by beautiful gardens. These were laid out in complicated patterns, their gravel paths and sunny flower beds being hedged with lavender or box shrubs. The most impressive buildings of all were the royal palaces, built near the capital. They were decorated by the finest craftsmen in Europe. Hampton Court, in Surrey, was built by Thomas Wolsey. He offered it to Henry VIII as a present, when it looked as though he might be falling from favour.

OAK AND PLASTER

In Tudor country houses and palaces, there were wooden panels and great carved staircases. Furniture include cupboards and heavy chests of oak. Ceilings were often decorated with raised plaster patterns, which were sometimes picked out in bold colours. Rich tapestries on the walls might show scenes of hunting or woodland views. Fireplaces were enormous, leading to high, ornate chimney pots.

Feather beds were enclosed by a carved four-poster frame, hung with heavy curtains.

🏵 **1538**
Building begins of Nonsuch royal palace in Surrey

🏵 **1540**
The astronomical clock installed at Hampton Court palace

🏵 **1553**
Longleat House is built in Witlshire, southern England

🏵 **1572**
A royal firework display is staged at Warwick Castle

15

Henry VIII studied music as a boy. He later composed religious music and popular songs.

TIME, SUN AND EARTH

The ingenious clock at Hampton Court was made for Henry VIII by Nicholas Oursian, in 1540. It not only tells the time, but shows the month, the number of days since the year began, high tides, phases of the Moon and signs of the zodiac. It also shows the Sun moving around the Earth. A book by the Polish astronomer Nicolaus Copernicus, explaining that actually it is the Earth which moves around the Sun, was not published until 1543.

The Tudor rulers moved from one palace to another during the year. Hampton Court was their favourite.

COURT AND CULTURE

In the 1500s there was a great renewal of interest in learning, in the civilizations of ancient Greece and Rome, in painting and sculpture and in invention. This period, called the Renaissance or 'rebirth', began in Italy, but its influence was also felt in northern Europe. The Tudor rulers were well educated and intelligent. Artists such as the great German painter Hans Holbein the Younger came to the English court.

Henry VIII and his courtiers loved music, dancing and playing royal or 'real' tennis, a version of the game which was played in an indoor court. They also loved to hunt deer in the royal parks and forests.

16

⊠ **1485**
Henry Tudor flies red dragon
standard at battle of Bosworth

⊠ **1523**
Poets gather at Caerwys for
an eisteddfod.

⊠ **1536**
The first Act of Union. Wales
is annexed by England

⊠ **1542**
The second Act of Union
becomes law

⊠ **1547**
The first book to be printed
in the Welsh language

WALES UNDER THE TUDORS

WALES during the reign of the Tudors was still mostly a land of farms and villages, of windmills and water wheels. Women spun and wove their own cloth. Few towns had more than 2,000 inhabitants. There was little industry, although coal was being mined in South Wales during the reign of Elizabeth I. Ships traded with Ireland, with other parts of Great Britain, France and Spain.

WELSH CONNECTIONS

Henry VII was of Welsh descent and fought under a red dragon standard at the battle of Bosworth. The green and white background on the modern Welsh flag represents the family colours of the Tudors. During the reign of Henry VII, many fortune-seekers arrived in London from Wales. The Seisyllt family, who came from the Welsh borders, became one of the most powerful families in Tudor England, changing their name to Cecil.

A stained glass window in the church at Penmynydd in North Wales recalls that this was the ancestral home of the Tudor family. The window is decorated with the Tudor rose emblem and symbols of royal power.

This fine map of Wales was published in 1573, during the reign of Elizabeth I. It was made by the cartographer Humphrey Llwyd who was born in Denbigh, North Wales, in about 1527. He was educated at Oxford University and died in 1568. The place names are shown in three languages – Latin, English and Welsh.

⊠ **1567**
The Book of Common Prayer
is published in Welsh

⊠ **1571**
The foundation of Jesus
College in Oxford, England

⊠ **1573**
Humphrey Llwyd publishes
his map of Wales

⊠ **1584**
Roman Catholic campaigner
Richard Gwyn is hanged

⊠ **1588**
Translation of the Bible into
Welsh by William Morgan

17

SCHOLARS AND BISHOPS

William Morgan, born in 1545, was the first to translate the whole of the Bible into Welsh. He was a scholar who understood Latin, Greek and Hebrew. He died at St Asaph, North Wales, in 1604.

In 1571 Hugh Price, an expert in Church law from Brecon, founded Jesus College, in Oxford, England, for Welsh students. Over the ages it kept its special links with Wales.

After 1588, students would have been able to read the Bible for the first time in the Welsh language. The brilliant translation was by William Morgan, who in 1595 became Bishop of Llandaff. Morgan's masterpiece helped to shape the Welsh language and keep it alive into modern times.

THE ACTS OF UNION

The Tudors may have been proud of their Welsh ancestors, but as rulers of England they demanded total control of their lands. By the Acts of Union, passed in 1536 and 1542, Wales and the Marcher lordships were annexed, or taken over, by England. In doing this, Henry VIII took the first step towards creating a United Kingdom. Welsh law and Welsh customs were to be abolished. No Welsh person could hold public office unless they could speak English, a ruling which excluded 95 percent of the population. Otherwise, Welsh citizens did now have equal rights with English citizens before the law, and were represented in the English parliament.

Roofs and gables
The roof was supported by massive wooden beams and tiled with slate. The stepped design of the gable ends was copied from Flanders.

Servants' bedrooms
Servants slept in male and female dormitories in the attic.

The cellars
Barrels of ale and wine were stored in the basement.

The great chamber
The chief reception room had decorated plasterwork, showing Tudor roses and coats of arms.

One of the finest Tudor town houses in Britain survives at Plas Mawr, in Conwy, North Wales. It was built in 1577 for a wealthy local gentleman named Robert Wynn.

Preparing food
On the ground floor was the kitchen, the pantry and the brewhouse.

18

❌ **1547**
Somerset becomes Protector
as Edward VI is still a boy

❌ **1549**
First Book of Common Prayer
is printed in English

❌ **1549**
Rebellions in Cornwall and
East Anglia

❌ **1550**
Somerset is overthrown,
replaced by Warwick

❌ **1553**
Edward VI dies, Lady Jane
Grey declared queen

PROTESTANT OR CATHOLIC?

Edward VI was a sickly boy, who died young.

Henry VIII died in 1547. Would England become Protestant or Roman Catholic? Living through the years that followed was like riding a see-saw, as rulers swung from the one faith to the other. There were fierce struggles between powerful nobles. Many people suffered economic hardship.

THE BOY KING

Edward VI was just 10 when he came to the throne. The son of Henry VIII and Jane Seymour, he was raised as a strict Protestant. He was very clever and learned Greek, Latin and French. His uncle Edward Seymour, Duke of Somerset, governed as Lord Protector in his place. However Somerset was overthrown and executed in 1552, to be replaced by John Dudley, Duke of Northumberland. Edward VI died from tuberculosis in 1553.

THE GRAMMAR SCHOOLS

Now that there were no more monks to carry out teaching work, schools became more and more important. Many new schools were named after the Tudors, others after the rich merchants who funded them. It was mostly boys who received formal schooling. The school day lasted from six in the morning until four or five in the afternoon. Pupils learned to write using slates. They learned to read and did sums and were beaten if they made mistakes. A lot of the time was spent learning Latin grammar, so these were known as 'grammar schools'.

The grammar school in Stratford-upon-Avon was named after Edward VI. Its most famous pupil in Tudor times was a young lad called William Shakespeare.

1553	1554	1554	1555	1558	19
Jane Grey is imprisoned. Mary I becomes queen	Sir Thomas Wyatt's rebellion fails. Jane Grey is executed	Mary I of England marries King Philip II of Spain	Persecution of Protestants begins. 300 executed	England loses Calais, its last French possession	

QUEEN FOR NINE DAYS

The Duke of Northumberland had persuaded the young king to make his daughter-in-law, Lady Jane Grey, heir to the throne of England. She was crowned queen in 1553, but within just nine days had been forced from the throne by the supporters of the rightful heir, Mary Tudor. Jane was imprisoned. After Sir Thomas Wyatt the Younger started a rebellion in her name, she was beheaded in the Tower of London in 1554, at the age of 16.

Jane was a quiet, intelligent girl, a Protestant and a great grand-daughter of Henry VII. Against her will, she became a pawn in a deadly game of power politics.

BLOODY MARY

Mary Tudor was the daughter of Henry VIII and Catherine of Aragon. Her father had forced her to sign a document stating that his marriage to her mother had been illegal. Mary remained a very unhappy woman for most of her life. She was a Roman Catholic and in 1554 married King Philip II of Spain. He spent little more than a year in England and the marriage was very unpopular. Mary began to bring back the Catholic faith. During the last three years of her reign, 300 leading Protestants were burned alive. This earned her the nickname of 'Bloody Mary'.

PRINCESS ELIZABETH

Mary I had a young half-sister, the daughter of Henry VIII and Anne Boleyn. Princess Elizabeth loved learning as well as playing music, dancing and riding. She was raised as a Protestant and this aroused the suspicion of Mary, who imprisoned her for a time. Elizabeth had to tread very, very carefully. However when Mary died without a child, in 1558, it was Elizabeth who became Queen of England.

Protestant churchmen who went to their death in the years 1555-1556 included Hugh Latimer, Nicholas Ridley and Archbishop Thomas Cranmer.

20

⊠ **1558**
Elizabeth I becomes Queen of
England

⊠ **1558**
William Cecil is appointed
Secretary of State

⊠ **1559**
The Church of England is
established

⊠ **1569**
Roman Catholic rebellion led
by northern earls

⊠ **1570**
Pope expels Elizabeth I from
the Roman Catholic Church

THE RED QUEEN

ELIZABETH, pale-skinned with flaming red hair, was crowned Queen of England in January 1559, dressed in heavy robes of gold and ermine fur. She was 25 years old. The new queen was warmly welcomed by the people, who longed for an end to religious strife and struggles for power.

STATESMEN AND SPIES

During the reign of Mary I, Elizabeth had learned how to survive in a world of plots and intrigue. As a queen, she possessed all the diplomatic and political skills that Mary had lacked. She surrounded herself with cunning statesmen such as William Cecil (who became Lord Burleigh) and set up a secret service under Sir Francis Walsingham. Elizabeth, like her father, enjoyed power and would let nobody stand in her way.

Although Elizabeth I never married, she had her favourite courtiers, such as Robert Dudley, Earl of Leicester (left), Christopher Hatton and, until they quarrelled, Robert Devereux, Earl of Essex.

Elizabeth I was much loved, and knew how to win public approval. However when she was crossed, she showed a fierce temper.

THE VIRGIN QUEEN

Who would the new queen marry? The throne of England was a rich prize. Elizabeth kept everyone guessing, playing off one suitor against another in order to gain political advantage. In the end, she married no one. She said that she was already married – to the English people.

Elizabeth I left no heir to the throne and so became known as the Virgin Queen. The newly formed North American colony of Virginia was named in her honour.

GLORIANA

Elizabeth I ruled over a glittering court. It was like a continuous dramatic performance, in which all eyes were drawn to her. She is said to have owned over 1,000 dresses. Courtiers competed for her approval and greatly feared falling from favour.

Elizabeth I inspired a great poetical work by Edmund Spenser, called *The Faerie Queene*. Characters in the book, which was written between 1590 and 1596, were meant to represent virtues and vices. Elizabeth is called Gloriana, the ideal queen.

At the court of Elizabeth I both men and women wore starched collars called ruffs. Later in her reign, women wore wide skirts stretched over hoops called farthingales.

Elizabeth's signature was scrawled across the page in ink, with a quill pen. The R stands for regina, which is Latin for 'queen'. The loops are intended to prevent any one else adding an extra message to the bottom of the document.

AT HOME AND ABROAD

The court moved around the country, making royal 'progresses'. Elizabeth's hosts had to spend a fortune on her entertainment and food. These journeys helped Elizabeth find out what was going on in her kingdom and made her aware of any local problems or needs. It also showed off her power and authority. Elizabeth I could speak Latin, French and Italian fluently, and she also knew ancient Greek and some Spanish. She spoke to foreign ambassadors directly – and often very forcibly – in protection of English trading interests.

Large areas of land were set aside as royal parks and forests. The queen and her courtiers would attend stag hunts, breaking off to enjoy open-air picnics and entertainments.

22

■ 1494
The body of English law now
applies in all Ireland

■ 1504
The Earls of Kildare
(Fitzgeralds) control Ireland

■ 1534
Rebellion in Ireland led by
Lord Offaly

■ 1557
Mary I starts 'plantation' in
Laois and Offaly

■ 1573
Elizabeth starts 'plantation' of
Ulster

IRELAND REBELS

D URING the early Tudor period, the most powerful
people in Ireland belonged to an old Norman
family, the Fitzgeralds. As Earls of Kildare, Gerald
Mór (1478–1513) and Gerald Óg (1513–1534) came to
control most of the country. England was happy for the
Fitzgeralds to look after the royal interests in Ireland – but
only so long as they did not challenge English rule.

*This well-to-do
lady comes from
the Pale, the English-
speaking area around
Dublin.*

RELIGIOUS DIVISIONS

The political divisions of Ireland
were further complicated when
Henry VIII broke with the
Roman Church. The Irish-
speaking Gaels remained faithful
to Rome. Of the rest, some
remained loyal to the king, but
could not accept him as head of
the Church. Others accepted the
new order, and did well for
themselves, as they profited from
wealth seized from the Church.

In 1534 the Fitzgeralds
declared themselves for the
Pope. One of them – Thomas,
Lord Offaly – rose up against
Henry VIII but was defeated by
an English army.

*In the Gaelic west, long-
haired mercenary soldiers,
the 'kern', were armed with long
swords and daggers. Their home
villages were made up of simple
thatched houses, often grouped
around a fortified tower.*

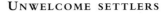

| 1579 | 1593 | 1601 | 1603 | 1607 | 23 |
| Rebellions in Munster and (1580) Leinster | Hugh O'Neill leads rebellion in Ulster | English defeat O'Neill's rebellion | Treaty of Mellifont confiscates lands of Irish nobles | Flight of the Earls. Irish nobles flee to mainland Europe | |

THE PIRATE QUEEN

During the 1560s, shipping off the west coast of Ireland came under attack from a fleet of pirate ships. These were based in Clew Bay, where they could hide out amongst a maze of small islands. The fleet was commanded by an Irish noble woman called Gràinne ni Mhàille, or Grace O'Malley. In 1593 she negotiated a pardon from Elizabeth I, in person.

Grace O'Malley's pirate galleys attacked English and Irish ships. In 1557 she repelled an English attack on her stronghold.

UNWELCOME SETTLERS

Mary I may have been a Roman Catholic, but she supported an English policy of colonization or 'plantation' in Ireland. English settlers were 'planted' in Laois and Offaly, which were now to be known as Queen's County and King's County. Under Elizabeth I, Irish colonization became a religious drive, with Protestant nobles eager to grab land from the Catholic Irish. Elizabeth I 'planted' Ulster, in the north. Most early plantation attempts failed, but they started a process which proved to be disastrous for Ireland.

In 1607 Hugh O'Neill fled to the Netherlands, which were at that time ruled by Spain. He died in Rome in 1616.

REBELLION AND FLIGHT

The most serious Irish rebellion broke out in Ulster, in 1595. It was led by Hugh O'Neill, Earl of Tyrone. In 1598 he led a victory over the English at the battle of the Yellow Ford, but was himself defeated by 1601. By the Treaty of Mellifont, signed in 1603, vast areas of land were seized from the Irish. By 1607 the Irish nobles were in despair. Many cut their losses and fled to mainland Europe – the 'Flight of the Earls'.

1504	1505	1513	1538	1542
James IV marries Margaret Tudor	James IV starts to build a Scottish navy	James IV killed by English at the battle of Flodden	James V marries Mary of Guise, a French Catholic	James V dies. He is followed by his infant daughter Mary

24

MARY, QUEEN OF SCOTS

THE Stewart family ruled Scotland for over 340 years. Many of their early kings came to the throne in their childhood, and this allowed powerful Lowlands families, highland chieftains and Lords of the Isles to grasp power for themselves. There were court plots, royal murders and endless wars with the English. Scotland's closest links were with France, which kept to the 'auld alliance'.

THE STEWART COURT

The greatest of the Stewart kings was James IV, who became king in 1488. He married Margaret Tudor, sister of Henry VIII. His court attracted poets and musical composers such William Dunbar and Robert Carver. James IV built new palaces and a fleet of warships. Tragically, he was killed at the Battle of Flodden in 1513. He was the last Scottish king to speak the Gaelic language.

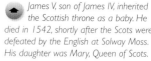
James V, son of James IV, inherited the Scottish throne as a baby. He died in 1542, shortly after the Scots were defeated by the English at Solway Moss. His daughter was Mary, Queen of Scots.

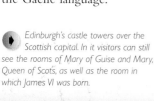
Edinburgh's castle towers over the Scottish capital. In it visitors can still see the rooms of Mary of Guise and Mary, Queen of Scots, as well as the room in which James VI was born.

SCOTTISH RULERS
House of Stewart

✤ Robert II	1371-1390
✤ Robert III	1390-1406
✤ James I	1406-1437
✤ James II	1437-1460
✤ James III	1460-1488
✤ James IV	1488-1513
✤ James V	1513-1542
✤ Mary (Stuart)	1542-1567
✤ James VI (I of England)	1567-1625

HOLYROODHOUSE

James IV and James V built a royal palace called Holyroodhouse in Edinburgh. It was here, in Queen Mary's apartments, that secretary David Rizzio was horribly murdered in 1566. His killers included William Ruthven and James Douglas, Earl of Morton.

◗ Holyroodhouse was built on the site of a medieval abbey founded by David I. The palace was repeatedly destroyed by the English. Much of it was rebuilt after the 1650s.

A QUEEN RETURNS

James V's widow, Mary of Guise, ruled as regent, for her daughter Mary was still a baby. A French Catholic, she soon clashed with the Protestants. The young queen was sent to the French court and raised as a Catholic. In 1558 she married the heir to the French throne, but her husband – and her mother – both died in 1560. Mary Stuart (as the family name was now spelt) returned to Scotland. In 1565 Mary married her cousin, Henry Darnley. It was a disastrous mistake.

IMPRISONED IN ENGLAND

Darnley became involved in a plot to murder Mary's Italian secretary, and was then murdered himself. Mary then married the suspected murderer, the Earl of Bothwell. Mary was forced off the throne and imprisoned. Her baby son James VI became king. Mary escaped and fled to her cousin, Elizabeth I. In England, however, she was held prisoner for 19 years. Elizabeth feared that Catholics would plot to put Mary on the English throne.

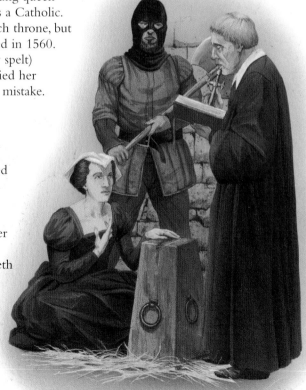

◗ The life of Mary, Queen of Scots ended tragically. The English secret service uncovered a Catholic plot and claimed that Mary was involved. She was beheaded at Fotheringay Castle in February 1587.

26

⊠ **1585**
England enters war between
the Dutch and Spanish

⊠ **1585**
Spanish ports attacked by
Francis Drake

⊠ **1585**
Spain confiscates English ships
in Spanish ports

⊠ **1586**
English and Dutch defeat
Spanish at battle of Zutphen

⊠ **1587**
Francis Drake raids Spanish
port of Cadiz

THE SPANISH ARMADA

I N May 1588 a massive invasion fleet or
'Armada' sailed from the port of Lisbon. It
was made up of 130 ships fitted with 2,500
guns. They carried 30,000 soldiers and sailors.
The ships included large warships called
galleons, armed merchant ships, galleys (which
used oars as well as sails) and supply vessels. This
great war fleet was bound for the English
Channel.

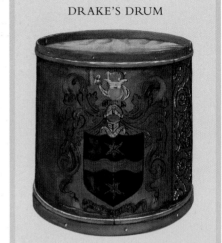

DRAKE'S DRUM

This drum was beaten during the
Armada crisis, when Sir Francis Drake
called his crew to action on the deck
of the *Revenge*.

 *When the English sea captain
Francis Drake carried out
illegal raids on Spanish shipping in
the Americas, Elizabeth I ignored
complaints from Spain. In 1587
Drake set fire to the Spanish port of
Cadiz. The raid was described as
'singeing the King of Spain's beard'.*

WHY DID THE ARMADA SAIL?

Spain had become the richest and most powerful country
in Europe. It was still ruled by King Philip II, former
husband of Mary I of England. From 1580 he was also
king of Portugal. The Netherlands too were under
Spanish rule, as were vast, newly discovered regions of the
Americas. When Dutch Protestants rose up against rule by
Catholic Spain, English armies were sent to help them. And
across the Atlantic Ocean, the English were fiercely
competing with the Spanish to grab the riches of the
Americas.

SEA DOGS FROM DEVON

Most of the great Elizabethan seafarers spoke English with
strong west-country accents. Francis Drake, John Hawkyns,
Humphrey Gilbert, Walter Raleigh and Richard Grenville
were all from Devon, in the southwest of England. Francis
Drake was a hero to the English and was knighted by
Elizabeth I. To the Spanish, who called him *El Draco*, he
was a common pirate.

⊠ **1588 May:**
Spanish Armada sets sail from
Lisbon

⊠ **1588 July:**
Spanish Armada defeated in
English Channel

⊠ **1589**
Francis Drake fails to
capture port of Lisbon

⊠ **1591**
Battle of Flores off the Azores.
Richard Grenville is killed

⊠ **1597**
A second Armada from Spain
is scattered by storms

27

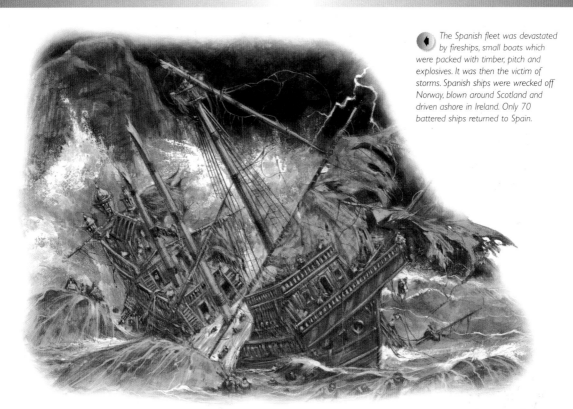

◀ *The Spanish fleet was devastated
by fireships, small boats which
were packed with timber, pitch and
explosives. It was then the victim of
storms. Spanish ships were wrecked off
Norway, blown around Scotland and
driven ashore in Ireland. Only 70
battered ships returned to Spain.*

IN PLYMOUTH AND TILBURY

As the Armada approached Cornwall, naval
squadrons were stationed along the Channel
coast, under the command of Lord Howard of
Effingham. Drake's ships lay in Plymouth
harbour. An army of 20,000 men was drawn
up at Tilbury, on the River Thames, as a Spanish
army from the Netherlands was expected to
invade the southeast. Elizabeth I rode out to
speak to the troops and steady nerves.

SCATTERED BY STORMS

The English ships sailed out to meet the
Armada. They had long-range guns and
chased the big galleons as they wallowed in
high seas, driven by westerly winds. Fighting
off Portland Bill and the Isle of Wight was
followed by an eight-hour sea battle off
Gravelines. The Armada was badly damaged.
It was now driven northwards and scattered
by roaring gales.

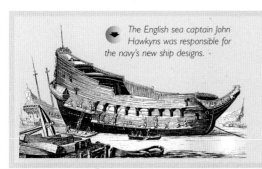

◀ *The English sea captain John
Hawkyns was responsible for
the navy's new ship designs.*

BUILDING A FLEET

Elizabeth I's new navy
was built at the royal
dockyards in Chatham,
Kent. The navy was still
small, having only 34
ships – although
merchant vessels could
also be used in warfare.

The old ships of the
Middle Ages, which were
really floating troop
carriers, were replaced by
new ships of oak. These
were nippier than the big
Spanish galleons – sleeker
and lower in the water.

28

1603	1604	1605	1606	1606
Union of English and Scottish thrones	The first English dictionary is published	Guy Fawkes arrested at the English parliament	Guy Fawkes and seven others are executed	The first version of the Union Flag is flown

TREASON·AND GUNPOWDER

I N her old age Elizabeth I was still riding, dancing and hunting, but her face was drawn and haggard. She died of pneumonia, at Richmond palace, in 1603. The throne now passed to James VI of Scotland, the protestant son of Mary, Queen of Scots, and descendant of Margaret Tudor. He was crowned James I of England.

This silver coin, minted in 1603-1604, was called a 'crown'. It shows James I on horseback and gives his name in Latin – Jacobus.

The first version of the Union Flag was flown from 1606 until 1801. It combined the English flag (a St George's cross, red on a white field) with the Scottish flag of St Andrew (a saltire or diagonal cross, white on a blue field).

AT THE COURT OF KING JAMES

The thrones of Scotland and England were now united, but in 1607 the English parliament rejected a full union of the two countries. James remained absent from Scotland for 14 years. He brought in harsh anti-Catholic laws, but they were never enough to satisfy the growing number of extreme protestants, or Puritans. People also resented the favours he gave his personal friends at court, such as Robert Carr, Earl of Somerset, and George Villiers, Duke of Buckingham.

Lancashire had major witch trials in 1612 and 1633.

A WITCH HUNT

Laws against witchcraft were passed in 1563 and 1604. There was public hysteria about so-called pacts with the devil and many poor, innocent women were accused of being witches. They were thrown into ponds, tortured and hanged. In 1645 a lawyer called Matthew Hopkins turned 'witchfinder', prowling East Anglia in search of people he could send to the gallows.

IN A COUNTRY COTTAGE

Life for working people in the countryside had improved since the Middle Ages. Even so, it was far from easy. Most cottages now had some furniture and some pots and pans. Bedsteads had sheets of coarse hemp, occasionally of linen. Fuel was hard to come by, as woodland was fast disappearing. Poor people often burnt peat or bracken in the hearth, for only the rich could afford coal.

RULERS OF GREAT BRITAIN AND IRELAND

House of Stuart

✠ James I of England (VI of Scotland)	1603–1625
✠ Charles I	1625–1649

Commonwealth and Protectorate

✠ Council of State	1649–1653
✠ Oliver Cromwell	1653–1658
✠ Richard Cromwell	1658–1659

House of Stuart

✠ Charles II	1660–1685
✠ James II of England (VII of Scotland)	1685–1688
✠ William III of Orange	1689–1702
✠ Mary II	1689–1694
✠ Anne	1702–1714

ANTI-SMOKING CAMPAIGN

The Spanish were the first Europeans to bring back tobacco from the Americas. In 1586 Francis Drake and Ralph Lane (the first governor of Virginia) presented Walter Raleigh with tobacco and a pipe. Soon it became the fashion to puff on a long pipe made of clay – much to the disgust of King James, who campaigned against this new tobacco habit.

King James failed in his bid to stop people smoking tobacco

THE GUNPOWDER PLOT

On the night of 4 November 1605, a search party was sent to Parliament buildings in London. A suspicious letter had been discovered. Was there a Catholic plot to blow up King James there, the following day? In the cellars, lantern light revealed barrels of gunpowder and one of the conspirators, Guy Fawkes. He was arrested, tortured and executed for treason along with seven others. His death is still celebrated each year on 5 November, with dummy 'guys' being burnt on bonfires. However some historians argue that the conspirators were set up – in order to discredit the Catholics.

Guy (or Guido) Fawkes was just one of the people accused of the murder plot. The leader was said to be Robert Catesby.

30

⊠ **1628**
Petition of Right increases
power of English Parliament

⊠ **1629**
Charles I starts rule without
Parliament (until 1640)

⊠ **1634**
Charles I brings in a tax called
ship money to fund the navy

⊠ **1637**
Attempt to force Scots to
use English form of worship

⊠ **1638**
The Covenant is signed in
Scotland

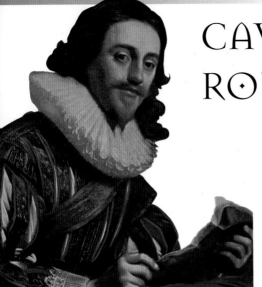

CAVALIERS AND ROUNDHEADS

O N 22 August 1642, King Charles I raised his standard at Nottingham. His enemy was not a foreign power, but forces loyal to the parliament of his own country. This was a Civil War, which would rage across England, Wales, Scotland and Ireland, dividing communities and even families.

Charles I reigned for 24 years. He married Princess Henrietta Maria of France and had six children. However his failure to come to terms with Parliament put the future of the monarchy at risk and cost him his life.

CHANGING TIMES

King James I of England (VI of Scotland) died in 1625. His son, Charles I, came to the throne of a country which was going through many changes. The power of the extreme Protestants, or Puritans, was growing and they were suspicious of his marriage with a Roman Catholic. The middle and lower classes of society were beginning to have more economic power. The country squires and landowners who were members of the House of Commons were demanding more say in running the country. Charles I treated them with disdain.

Civil War armies fought with swords, pikes, muskets and pistols. Royalist commanders, who often wore fancy clothes and long hair, were known as Cavaliers ('knights'). Supporters of Parliament were often Puritans, who wore plain clothes and cropped their heads. They were known as Roundheads.

COVENANTERS IN SCOTLAND

Charles I had little understanding of Scotland. The Scottish Church was Presbyterian – it was against having bishops. Charles I tried to force the Scots to follow English forms of worship. In 1638 the Scots drew up a petition, the National Covenant, rejecting his demands. Charles I went to war with the Covenanters in 1639 and 1640, but was forced to make peace. He had made enemies which, in the end, would cost him dearly.

A GROWING CRISIS

From 1629 to 1640 Charles I summoned no parliaments at all. He brought in unpopular taxes, which caused protests and unrest. In 1641 Parliament demanded that the king replace his ministers and bring in religious reforms. In 1642 Charles I forced his way into the House of Commons and attempted to arrest five Members of Parliament. He failed, and so went to war.

THE FIRST CIVIL WAR

The first battle took place at Edgehill in 1642. Both sides claimed to have won. In 1643 Parliament allied with the Scottish Covenanters and defeated the Royalists at Marston Moor in the following year. They were crushed again at Naseby, near Leicester, in 1645. In 1646, Charles I surrendered to the Scots.

Weapons are brandished and horses whinny as a battle of the Civil War is re-enacted. In 1645 a commander called Oliver Cromwell reorganized Parliament's forces. His New Model Army was efficient, ruthless and very successful.

ROADS AND COACHES

The roads tramped by Civil War armies were still muddy and potholed, but attempts were now being made to map them, improve them and carry out repairs.

The first stage coach service began in 1640.

THE SECOND CIVIL WAR

Charles I now tried to come to an agreement with the English Parliament, but failed. In 1647 he fled to the Isle of Wight. He made a secret deal with his former enemies in Scotland, promising them the reforms they desired. The Scots marched on England and there were Royalist risings in Wales, too. However all were defeated and by 1649 Charles was imprisoned.

32

⊠ **1649**
Charles I is executed in London

⊠ **1649**
A republic, or 'Commonwealth' is declared

⊠ **1649**
Government is by a Council of State

⊠ **1649**
The Levellers are defeated at Burford

⊠ **1651**
Scots crown Charles II king, but are defeated at Worcester

COMMONWEALTH

O N 30 January 1649, Charles I was marched from St James's Palace to Whitehall. It was a bitterly cold day in London, with flurries of snow. At one o'clock the king stepped to the scaffold, or execution platform. When the axe had fallen, his head was shown to the ranks of soldiers and the crowd.

THE KING IS DEAD

It was reported that although Charles I had been an unpopular king, a groan passed through the London crowd when he died. Ever since the Middle Ages, people had believed that kings ruled by the will of God. Charles I himself believed in this 'divine right' of kings. He kept silent throughout his trial. News of the king's death spread like wildfire through the British Isles and mainland Europe. To many people, it was simply unbelievable.

A LORD PROTECTOR

The nation was now a republic, or 'Commonwealth'. Parliament ruled the land instead of a king or queen. It governed through a Council of State, made up of 40 members. However as far as the army was concerned, Parliament was much too cautious in its reforms. In 1653 power was handed over to one man, Oliver Cromwell, who was appointed Lord Protector. His rule was harsh but effective. He attempted to bring in military rule, and in 1556 he was even offered the crown.

Charles I died bravely, within sight of the Parliament he despised.

George Fox believed that all people were equal and that nobody should fight wars.

THE QUAKERS

In 1646 a Puritan called George Fox preached a new kind of faith. He called upon his followers to 'quake at the word of the Lord'. They became known as 'Quakers', or The Society of Friends. The Friends worshipped God in silence, with no priests or prayers or churches. Many of them were imprisoned for their beliefs or forced to flee the country.

NO MORE FUN!

Many of Cromwell's supporters were Puritans. The only joy that they could accept was through religious worship. Dancing and theatre were banned. Meat or ale could not be consumed on a Sunday, and even Christmas Day was no longer to be celebrated with plum puddings and merry-making.

Playing cards were believed to be the work of the Devil.

WHAT KIND OF REVOLUTION?

The English revolution was controlled by landowners and wealthy merchants, but its footsoldiers were poor people, craft workers, small farmers and tradesmen. Some of these formed a political movement called the Levellers. They demanded true democracy (rule by the people), but were quickly crushed by Cromwell in 1649. In 1650 an even more radical group was broken up. These True Levellers or 'Diggers' demanded equality for all and the common ownership of land.

Oliver Cromwell was a squire from the Huntingdon countryside. He made sure that no ruler could ever again afford to ignore the wishes of Parliament.

TUMBLEDOWN DICK

Warfare did not come to an end with the Common-wealth. In 1651 Charles I's son was crowned Charles II in Scotland. The Scots marched south, but were defeated and Charles II fled abroad. From 1652-1654 Britain fought the Netherlands (now a free and increasingly wealthy nation) over trade. Oliver Cromwell died on a stormy night in 1658. His son Richard (known as 'Tumbledown Dick') was made Lord Protector, but had little taste for power. The revolution was over.

34

⊠ 1609	⊠ 1626	⊠ 1633	⊠ 1641	⊠ 1647
Plantation of six counties of Ulster	Charles I unofficially accepts Catholic worship in Ireland	Wentworth (later Earl of Strafford) becomes Governor	Strafford executed for treason. Rising in Ulster	Dublin yields to Parliament in the Civil War

DROGHEDA AND AFTER

MORE and more lands belonging to Irish Catholics were seized and given over to Protestant English and Scottish settlers. This continuing policy of 'plantation' was supported by the Dublin parliament. In 1628 Charles I decided to allow Roman Catholic worship to continue alongside the Protestant Church, but this infuriated Ireland's Protestants.

WENTWORTH AND ULSTER

In 1633 Charles I appointed a new man to govern Ireland. He was Thomas Wentworth, who later became Earl of Strafford. Wentworth's only aim was to increase royal power in Ireland. He managed to earn the hatred of Catholics and Protestants alike. He drew up plans for further plantation. As a result, violence broke out in Ulster in 1641 and soon spread far and wide. Perhaps 2,000 Protestants were killed and many more were stripped and chased naked from their homes.

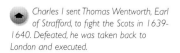

Charles I sent Thomas Wentworth, Earl of Strafford, to fight the Scots in 1639-1640. Defeated, he was taken back to London and executed.

A ROMAN LIFELINE

Irish Catholics were supported by the Church in Rome, which trained priests for work in Ireland. Political support also came from Roman Catholic countries in Europe. When Oliver Cromwell came to Ireland, he blamed Catholic priests for all the country's problems. Many of them were murdered by his troops.

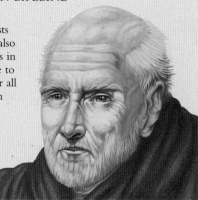

Luke Wadding was a monk who founded St Isidore's College in Rome in 1625. He worked tirelessly to keep the Roman Catholic faith alive in Ireland.

FROM WAR TO WAR

The tragic fate of the Protestant settlers in Ulster was used to whip up extreme anti-Catholic feelings in Britain. In 1642 an army of Scottish Covenanters arrived in Ulster to defend the Scottish Protestants who had settled there. A Catholic army was formed too by Owen Roe O'Neill. An alliance was made between Old English royalists and Irish Catholics, but there were bitter divisions.

CROMWELL INVADES

Events were overtaken by the Civil War in Britain. Oliver Cromwell invaded Ireland in August 1649, with a battle-hardened army of Puritan troops. They hated all Roman Catholics and wanted revenge for the events of 1641. Cromwell besieged and sacked Drogheda, killing no fewer than 2,500 people. A massacre at Wexford claimed a further 2,000 lives. Perhaps a quarter of all Irish Catholics were killed during this savage campaign. Cromwell followed it up in 1652 by seizing Catholic lands and granting them to his soldiers and followers. He sowed seeds of hatred which still bear fruit today.

The River Shannon became a new frontier after Oliver Cromwell's invasion. Irish Catholic landowners were told that they had until 1 May 1654 to resettle west of the Shannon.

Oliver Cromwell sacked Drogheda in September 1649. Some of the defenders were burnt alive in a church he set on fire. Cromwell's official report called the massacre 'a righteous judgement of God upon these barbarous wretches'.

36

⊠ 1660
Samuel Pepys starts to write his diary

⊠ 1660
The monarchy is restored. Charles II returns

⊠ 1661
The Church of England is established

⊠ 1662
Tea drinking becomes fashionable

⊠ 1665
The Second Anglo-Dutch War (until 1667)

THE RESTORATION

G REAT Britain and Ireland had a king again, Charles II. In 1660 Parliament had finally asked him to return from exile and be crowned. In return, Charles had to agree to recognize Parliament and the limits of his power. There was great rejoicing as he entered London on his thirtieth birthday. Oliver Cromwell's remains were seized from his tomb in Westminster Abbey and publicly hanged from the gallows at Tyburn.

THE WORLD OF POLITICS
During the reign of Charles II, the way in which the British political system was organized became rather more like the one in use today. From 1667–1673, Charles II began to consult with a group of ministers instead of just one. These were rather like the Cabinet in modern times. They were known as the 'Cabal', because of their initials (Clifford, Ashley, Buckingham, Arlington, Lauderdale). The world 'cabal' is still used to describe a small, powerful group of people. The first political parties were formed in the 1680s. They were known as Tories and Whigs.

THE DIARY OF SAMUEL PEPYS

Samuel Pepys wrote freely about his private life and everyday pastimes.

In January 1660 a Londoner called Samuel Pepys began to write a diary. It was written in a secret code. Pepys offers us a lively look at how people lived in the 1660s. He knew many famous people and was mixed up in all sorts intrigues at the court. He describes the news stories of his day, as when Dutch warships sailed up the River Thames.

◀ *Nell Gwyn began her career as an orange-seller. She became a famous actress, much admired by Samuel Pepys, and was a lover of the king himself.*

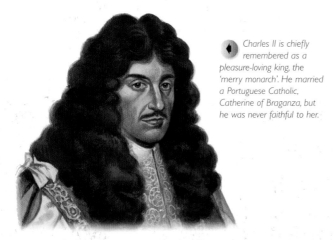

◀ *Charles II is chiefly remembered as a pleasure-loving king, the 'merry monarch'. He married a Portuguese Catholic, Catherine of Braganza, but he was never faithful to her.*

RELIGIOUS FREEDOM?
In 1662 the Church of England was recognized as the official Church. In the following year Charles II declared that both Catholics and Puritans would be free to worship in their own way. However, he was forced to end this offer in 1673, when Parliament ruled that Catholics could not hold public office.

⊠ **1667**
The 'Cabal' ministry is formed
by Charles II

⊠ **1672**
The Third Anglo-Dutch War
(until 1674)

⊠ **1678**
John Bunyan writes first
part of *Pilgrim's Progress*

⊠ **1678**
A 'Popish Plot' is faked by
Titus Oates. Catholics
executed

⊠ **1685**
Charles II has a fit and dies,
aged 55

37

A MERRY DANCE

After the Restoration, the English began
to enjoy life again. Theatres re-opened in
1660. Female parts in plays were now
taken by actresses, who became as
popular as film stars would be 300 years
later. Dancing was never more popular,
from the royal court to the village
maypole. Women wore make-up and
fancy dresses. Fashionable men wore
long, curled wigs. There were river trips,
fireworks, processions and fairs. In the
1660s and 1670s it became fashionable
to drink new beverages – coffee and tea.

THE PLOT THAT NEVER WAS

There was growing anti-Catholic
hysteria in England. In 1678 an English
spy called Titus Oates claimed that
Catholics were plotting to kill the king.
He had actually made the whole story
up, but 35 Catholics were executed
because of this 'Popish Plot'.

*This painting shows Charles II at a ball in the
Hague, in the Netherlands. His dancing
partner is his sister Mary, Princess of Orange (1631-
1660), whose son came to the British throne as
William III in 1688.*

*During Stuart times, the climate was colder than
today. Often, the River Thames froze solid. 'Frost Fairs'
were held on the ice and people practised ice-skating – a
sport recently brought in from the Netherlands.*

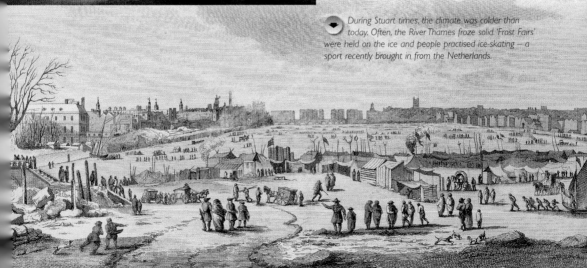

38

⊠ 1628
William Harvey's theories on
blood circulation

⊠ 1631
Death of the poet John
Donne

⊠ 1631
Anthony van Dyck is court
painter to Charles I

⊠ 1651
Thomas Hobbes writes about
politics and philosophy

⊠ 1662
Chemist Robert Boyle's
research into gases

GREAT MINDS

THE 1600s was an age of exploration and discovery. The old ways were challenged and knocked down. This exciting new world was reflected in literature, the arts, in philosophy and especially in science. In 1660 the Royal Society of London was founded to encourage learning. Leading members included Robert Boyle, Samuel Pepys and Isaac Newton.

Paradise Lost, one of the greatest works of English literature, was published by the English poet John Milton in 1667. During the Civil War, Milton was a keen supporter of Parliament. He became blind in middle age.

METAPHYSICAL POETS

In the 1600s many English poets broke away from the forms of poetry which had been popular in Elizabethan times. These 'metaphysical' poets included John Donne, George Herbert, Richard Crashaw and Andrew Marvell. They used unusual and sometimes complicated images, some of them taken from new discoveries in science and geography.

COURT MUSICIANS AND PAINTERS

In the 1630s the great Flemish painters Peter Paul Rubens and Anthony van Dyck came to the court of Charles I, as did the Dutch painter Peter Lely in the 1640s. The English musical composer Henry Purcell wrote the first English opera in 1689 and music for the coronations of James II of England (VII of Scotland).

THE PHILOSOPHERS

Thomas Hobbes (1588-1679) was a keen royalist. He wrote about politics and the human mind. John Locke (1632-1704) argued that governments ruled only with the agreement of the people. If they broke faith, they deserved to be overthrown.

The English scientist Robert Hooke used the newly invented microscope to study the structure of plants and chemicals. His Micrographia was published in 1665.

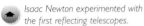 Isaac Newton experimented with the first reflecting telescopes.

William Harvey was doctor to Charles I. His theories on blood circulation were ridiculed by many scientists of his day.

GRAVITY AND LIGHT

Isaac Newton was born in Lincolnshire in 1642 and studied at Cambridge University. He was a brilliant mathematician and became one of the greatest scientists the world has ever known. Newton studied the nature of light. He also described how the forces of gravity work – legend has it, after watching an apple fall from a tree.

SCIENCE, MEDICINE, ASTRONOMY

The new science was based on careful observation and experiments. In 1628 an English doctor called William Harvey became the first person to describe how the heart pumps blood around the body through arteries and veins. In 1654 the Irish scientist Robert Boyle came to Oxford University to study gases, vacuums and the burning process. An English mathematician called Edmond Halley became a great astronomer. The most famous comet is named after him, for in 1680 he accurately predicted that it would return to the Earth's skies every 76 years.

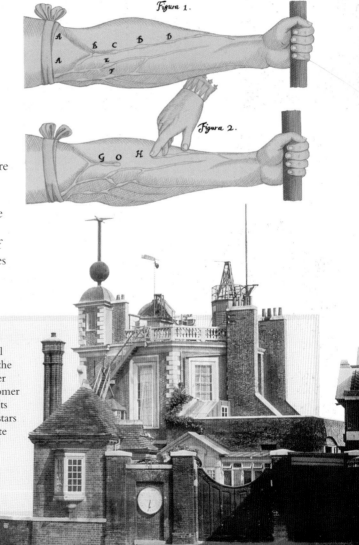

GREENWICH OBSERVATORY

In 1675 King Charles II founded a Royal Observatory at Greenwich, overlooking the River Thames. It was built by Christopher Wren and its first director was an astronomer from Derbyshire, called John Flamsteed. Its purpose was to observe the Sun, Moon, stars and planets, in order to help ships navigate across the oceans.

Today, the Royal Greenwich Observatory is a museum. However its work continues at Herstmonceux, Sussex, and at Cambridge.

⊠ **1665** June:
first reports of Great Plague
in London

⊠ **1665** October:
death toll from plague reaches
70,000

⊠ **1666** September:
fire breaks out in London

⊠ **1666** December:
end of the Great Plague

⊠ **1669**
Christopher Wren is
appointed Surveyor-General

⊙UT ⊙F THE ASHES

LONDON, by now a city of about half a million people, was hot and stifling on 6 June 1665. That was the day on which an outbreak of plague was reported in London. It caused little fuss at the time. Since the Black Death of the Middle Ages, the plague had returned time after time.

THE GREAT PLAGUE

This time, though, it was different. The bubonic plague, marked by foul swellings on the body, claimed 70,000 lives in just the first few months. As Londoners fled to the country, they brought the dreaded disease to villages and market towns. Survivors clutched bunches of sweet-smelling flowers to ward off the stench. The air itself seemed poisoned. An old nursery rhyme recalls plagues past: *Ring-a-ring o' roses, A pocket full of posies, Atishoo! Atishoo! We all fall down.*

● The cobbled streets and
alleys of London had
changed little since medieval
times. They still swarmed with
rats and their deadly fleas.

● Crosses were painted
on the doors of
houses stricken by plague.
Carts rumbled down the
streets, collecting corpses.

▣ 1675	▣ 1677	▣ 1694	▣ 1698	▣ 1710	41
Work starts on the rebuilding of St Paul's Cathedral, London	The Monument is completed in memory of the Great Fire	Christopher Wren builds new wings at Hampton Court	Work starts on the Royal Naval Hospital, Greenwich	The new St Paul's Cathedral is completed	

Many people took to the river to escape the heat and flames. After the fire, the old city with all its familiar landmarks was gone forever.

LONDON BURNS

After more than a year of plague, another disaster struck London. In the early hours of 2 September 1666, a fire started at a baker's in Pudding Lane. The flames were soon blazing over a wide area and continued to do so for five whole days, driven by the wind. Timber houses had to be blown up to stop the fire spreading. By the time it was over, the Great Fire had burnt down 13,200 houses, the old city gates, the Guildhall, 89 churches and the great cathedral of the City of London, St Paul's.

ASYLUM SEEKERS

The British Isles were not the only part of Europe to experience religious hatred and conflict in the 1500s and 1600s. In France there were terrible wars between Roman Catholics and the Protestant followers of John Calvin, who were known as Huguenots. After 1598 Protestant rights were protected by the Edict of Nantes, but during the reign of King Louis XIV many Huguenots were persecuted or forced to become Catholics. In 1685 the Edict of Nantes was cancelled, and 400,000 Huguenots fled the country. Many of these sought refuge in London. France's loss was England's gain, for many were hard-working weavers and skilled workers.

REBUILT IN STONE

Perhaps the Great Fire was a blessing in disguise. The old, rat-infested wooden houses were burnt to the ground. An architect was chosen to rebuild the capital. His name was Christopher Wren. Soon the streets were being widened and fine new houses were being built of stone. Wren built 52 new churches, of which 24 may still be seen today.

Wren's masterpiece was the new St Paul's Cathedral. Its great dome remained the chief landmark of London for 300 years.

42

⊠ **1685**
James VII of Scotland (II of England) becomes king

⊠ **1685**
The Monmouth rebellion and the Bloody Assizes

⊠ **1688** July:
William of Orange invited to become king

⊠ **1688** December:
James is overthrown

⊠ **1689**
William III and Mary II rule jointly

JAMES, WILLIAM AND MARY

CHARLES II died in February 1685. He was followed as king by his brother, who became James VII of Scotland and II of England. James was a Roman Catholic and this dismayed the Protestants. Many of these belonged to the more radical political party, the Whigs. They had had enough of Stuart kings who showed little regard for the wishes of the people.

Rebel fighters gathered at Sedgemore, Somerset, in support of Monmouth's rebellion. They were defeated by forces loyal to King James.

BLOODY ASSIZES

In June 1685 the Protestant James, Duke of Monmouth, a son of Charles II born outside marriage, landed in Lyme Regis, in southern England. He claimed the throne, but was defeated in July at Sedgemoor and executed. His followers were dealt with savagely by a judge called George Jeffreys, in a series of trials called the Bloody Assizes. A death sentence was passed on 320 people and 840 more were sold into slavery. It was a bitter start to the reign.

THE GLORIOUS REVOLUTION

By 1688 leading politicans had decided on a drastic plan. They invited the Dutch ruler, William of Orange, to become king. He was a Protestant and married to Mary, the king's daughter. William landed at Torbay in Devon and gained rapid support. James fled to France and it was agreed that William III and Mary II would rule jointly. This change of power became known as the Glorious Revolution.

A BILL OF RIGHTS

The most important outcome of the revolution was a Bill of Rights, passed in December 1689. This made it very clear that Parliament was now the chief governing body in the land, and that the power of kings and queens was strictly limited.

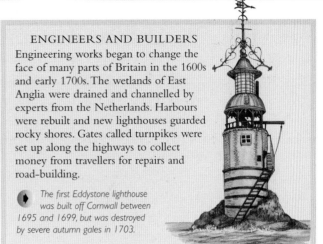

ENGINEERS AND BUILDERS

Engineering works began to change the face of many parts of Britain in the 1600s and early 1700s. The wetlands of East Anglia were drained and channelled by experts from the Netherlands. Harbours were rebuilt and new lighthouses guarded rocky shores. Gates called turnpikes were set up along the highways to collect money from travellers for repairs and road-building.

The first Eddystone lighthouse was built off Cornwall between 1695 and 1699, but was destroyed by severe autumn gales in 1703.

James's attempt to regain his throne finally ended in a pitched battle with William of Orange on the south bank of the River Boyne, on 1 July 1690. 'King Billy's' victory is still celebrated by the Protestant 'Orangemen' of Northern Ireland today, who see it as an important turning point in the history of the Union.

SCOTLAND AND IRELAND

William and Mary did not enjoy an easy reign. The Highland Scots rose up in support of James. Their leader was John Graham of Claverhouse, Viscount Dundee, a persecutor of the Covenanters. They won the battle of Killiecrankie in May 1689, but Dundee was killed and the rising failed. James now landed with French troops in Ireland, trying to regain the throne. William too led an army into Ireland, reinforced with Ulster Protestants. They met at the battle of the Boyne in 1690 and James was defeated.

MASSACRE AT GLENCOE

At this bleak spot, Glencoe in Stratchclyde, 37 members of the MacDonald clan were massacred in 1692. William III demanded that all the clans in the Scottish Highlands swear an oath of loyalty. They obeyed, but MacIan MacDonald of Glencoe signed late, due to a misunderstanding. Troops sealed off the ends of the glen, while others, billeted in MacDonald homes, carried out a brutal attack. They were commanded by Campbells, old enemies of the Macdonalds.

☒ 1668
Henry Morgan leads buccaneer army on Spanish Main

☒ 1671
Irish adventurer Thomas Blood tries to steal Crown Jewels

☒ 1684
Highwayman John Nevison hanged in York

☒ 1695
Pirate Henry Avery captures flagship of the Moghul emperor

☒ 1700s
Increase in taxes leads to smuggling around coasts of British Isles

A ROGUES' GALLERY

GALLOWS were a familiar sight to travellers through the British Isles in the 1600s and 1700s. The corpses of those who had been hanged were left to rot, swinging in the wind. Their eyes were pecked out by crows. Gallows often stood at crossroads, as a warning to highway robbers or sheep-stealers. They were erected at Tilbury docks, in London, too, as a grim reminder to would-be pirates as they sailed down the River Thames and out to sea.

SMUGGLERS ON THE COAST

People who lived in fishing villages around the coasts of the British Isles had always raided shipwrecks for cargoes and timber. About three hundred years ago they found a new source of income – smuggling. In order to pay for foreign wars being fought at that time, the government greatly increased the taxes on imported goods. Smugglers would meet up with merchant ships out at sea and run untaxed cargoes ashore in small boats, hiding them in caves or cellars. The illegal brandy, tobacco or silk was often sold on to the local squire – or even to the parson – at a handsome profit.

MARY READ AND ANNE BONNY

Mary Read was an English girl who dressed herself up as a young man in order to join the English army. She married a Flemish soldier. When he died, she sailed off to the Caribbean, where she was captured by pirates. She joined forces with them, only to find an Irish woman, Anne Bonny, was already serving in the crew. The two fought fiercely under the command of Captain 'Calico' Jack Rackham, sailing out of the Bahamas. In 1720 Rackham and his crew were captured and hanged in Jamaica. The women were expecting babies and so they escaped the gallows, but Mary Read soon died anyway, of a fever.

While Anne Bonny and Mary Read fought for their lives, Calico Jack hid below decks.

☒ 1701
Captain William Kidd hanged
in London for piracy

☒ 1718
Pirate Edward Teach
(Blackbeard) killed

☒ 1719
Howell Davis and Bart
Roberts raid West African
coast

☒ 1720
Anne Bonny, Mary Read and
Jack Rackham on trial

☒ 1729
Dick Turpin takes up highway
robbery

45

ON THE HIGH SEAS

Piracy greatly increased between the 1630s and the 1720s. As European nations grabbed land and plunder around the world, independent adventurers, escaped slaves, mutineers and murderers were washed up on foreign shores. At first, the British were quite happy to leave the Caribbean pirates or 'buccaneers' alone – as long as they attacked the ships of their enemies. In 1668 a Welsh adventurer called Henry Morgan was commissioned to lead a buccaneer army against the Spanish. He ended up as deputy governor of a British colony, Jamaica. Bristol-born Edward Teach, the dreaded 'Blackbeard', had the governor of another British colony, North Carolina, in his pay. Once pirates began to prey upon British trade, many were hunted down and executed. Blackbeard was shot and beheaded in 1718 and his head displayed on a pole.

Highwaymen lurked in woods and on lonely heaths such as Hounslow, to the west of London.

European pirates sailed all over the world. Two Welsh pirates, Howell Davis and Bartholomew Roberts ('Black Bart') raided West Africa's Guinea Coast in 1719.

GENTLEMEN OF THE ROAD

Highwaymen held up stage coaches and robbed the travellers. A former soldier called John Nevison (known as 'Swift Nicks') only robbed the rich. He was sent to the gallows in York in 1684. The most famous highway robber of all was Dick Turpin, also hanged in York in 1739. He was a burglar, murderer, smuggler and horse-thief. The public loved to watch hangings and read the popular ballads written about the dreadful crimes that had been committed.

Stage coach guards carried heavy firearms called blunderbusses to protect their passengers.

ÏΠDEX

Look up subjects to be found in this book.
Illustrations are shown in *italic* print.

ACKNOWLEDGEMENTS

The publishers would like to thank the following sources for the use of their images:

Page 11 (T/R) Gillian Darley/Edifice/Corbis; 12 (T/R) Francis G.Mayer/Corbis, (B) Tim Hawkins/Eye Ubiquitous/Corbis; 13 (T/L) Historical Picture Archive/Corbis, (B/L) Michael Nicholson/Corbis; 15 (B/R) Michael Nicholson/Corbis; 16 (Both) Robert Williams/MAGMA; 17 (T/L) Robert Williams/MAGMA; 18 (B) Adam Woolfitt/Corbis; 19 (B) Bettmann/Corbis; 20 (T/R) National Portrait Gallery/Bridgeman Art Library, (B/L) Corbis; 21 (B/R) The Art Archive; 26 (B/L) Corbis; 27 (B/L) Mary Evans Picture Library; 28 (B) Bettmann/Corbis; 31 (B) Kit Houghton Photography/Corbis; 37 (T/L) The Royal Collection Her Majesty Queen Elizabeth 11, (B) Historical Picture Archive/Corbis; 39 (B/R) Scheufter Collection/Corbis; 43 (T/L) AFP/Corbis

All other photographs from MKP Archives

The publishers would like to thank the artists whose work appears in this book:

Martin Camm, Peter Dennis /Linda Rogers Associates, Nicholas Forder, Terry Gabbey/AFA, Sally Holmes, Richard Hook/Linden Artists, Kevin Maddison, Janos Marffy, Peter Sarson, Rob Sheffield, Guy Smith/Mainline, Studio Galante, Rudi Vizi, Mike White/Temple Rogers